Leaving Eden

LIANE STRAUSS was born in Queens, New York, and grew up in Bergen County, New Jersey. She is the author of *Frankie, Alfredo*, (Donut Press, 2009). Her work has appeared in the pamphlets *The Like Of It* (2005) and *Ask for It by Name* (2008). She has also been published in *The Hudson Review, The Iowa Review* and *Poetry Daily* and teaches literature and creative writing at Birkbeck College, The City Literary Institute and The Poetry School. She lives in North London with her two sons.

Also by Liane Strauss

PAMPHLETS
Frankie, Alfredo, (Donut Press, 2009)

Leaving Eden

by

LIANE STRAUSS

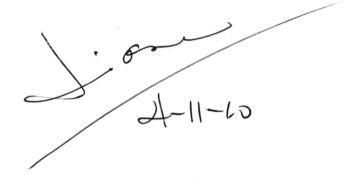

4-11-10

SALT

LONDON

PUBLISHED BY SALT PUBLISHING
Dutch House, 307–308 High Holborn, London WC1V 7LL United Kingdom

© Liane Strauss, 2010

The right of Liane Strauss to be identified as the
author of this work has been asserted by her in accordance
with Section 77 of the Copyright, Designs and Patents Act 1988.

Salt Publishing 2010

Printed in Great Britain by the MPG Books Group, Bodmin and King's Lynn

Typeset in Swift 9.5 / 13

ISBN 978 1 84471 446 9 paperback

1 3 5 7 9 8 6 4 2

for my parents
and
my children

Contents

Acknowledgements

My thanks to the editors of the following magazines and anthologies where some of these poems first appeared: *Buckle &*, *Cumberland Poetry Review*, *Future Welcome: The Moosehead Anthology X*, *The Georgia Review*, *The Hudson Review*, *The Liberal*, *Limelight*, *Lullwater Review*, *Magma*, *nth position*, *Poetry Review*, *Prairie Schooner*, *Rising*, *Salmagundi*, *The Sow's Ear Poetry Review* and *The Wolf*.

'Ditchdigger' was featured on *Poetry Daily* (2 June 2007). 'Childhood' was commended in the 2002 National Poetry Competition under the title 'Two Worlds'. 'Jigsaw World' won the 1999 Lullwater Prize for Poetry. '*Ceci n'est pas*' is available on the CD *Life Lines: Poets for Oxfam* edited by Todd Swift.

A number of these poems are included in the pamphlets *The Like of It* (Baring & Rogerson, 2005), *Ask for It by Name* (unfold press, 2008) and *Frankie, Alfredo,* (Donut Press, 2009), and on www.clivejames.com.

I am grateful to Karen Annesen, Simon Barraclough, Julia Bird, Andy Ching, Olivia Cole, Angela Conway, Isobel Dixon, Luke Heeley, Heather Holden, Simon Rees-Roberts and Roisin Tierney for their generosity, friendship and insight, which I have depended on in putting together this collection; to the late Michael Donaghy, for his kind encouragement; and especially to Diane Shooman for her inexhaustible enthusiasm and support from first to last.

Heaven never seals off all exits.

—Anonymous

Seduction

If people can dream together,
we dream together.
This is the way it always starts:
Out of the darkness of the streets that lie between us
and the river rising like a rampart raised to part the city
from its dreamed and dreaming counterpart
across the river—a darkness falling like the leaves
shed by the street lamps every evening dreaming
they shed light and keep the city from the river—
we find our way back to each other's side.
It doesn't take long.
It never does. Not in the dream
we dream together. I know you and you know me so well,
all we need to find each other is to sleep.
Inside this world more real than
real, we're always more and more awake.
It's how we dream it.
And maybe because it's a collaboration,
like a double negative,
what we end up with is the opposite of a dream,
where I'm about to tell you something,
but you already know it,
and you're about to tell me, since we dream together,
so that we stop and start and smile and stop again,
like two strangers in a doorway, until whatever it is that parts,
like dawn the lips of the curtain, like the last look,
tears us from each other's side—
you, half way across the labyrinth of dream and boulevard,

and me,
in my half, at the end of the street,
at the end of the night,
the street lamps stepping back in their own darkness,
where we started.

Round Trip

I tell you this, you tell me that.
We order tea, I watch your hand
reach for the bowl and hesitate,
as if what's sweet might turn to sand.

You tell me in exotic banter
of a dawn where flowers close.
Blossoms, I tell you, in deep winter
bloom, undaunted, out of loss.

The stops like stars ignite the tracks.
You touch my hair as if it's smoke
reflected in the window backwards
and the day that's come and gone.

Rumour

after Virgil

I'm not making this up.
I heard of a girl once who caught it
clear across a banquet hall
just from listening
to the confections of some confabulator.

Well, he was quite a talker,
and, like the champagne,
the more he poured, the more she frothed
until she was so intoxicated by the feeling
that she had to tell somebody
that she wanted to tell everybody.

She needn't have worried.
Like an airborne influenza, word got around.
The more it talked, the more it grew,
until at last and finally
it overwhelmed her. That's how it is.
In vino veritas, of love she flew.

Such things occur, I know, because
it was talk you took me with—
strange talk, and beautiful, and full of pity.
As I recall (I don't recall, I'm elaborating)
you went to my knees
one hundred proof, straight bourbon, bang
straight to my head like backwoods bootleg.

Ever since everything out of my mouth
is pure you. Your words keep
flaring up in me like fever, the stamp
of your expression on my tongue
like fog-bound battalion phantoms on an ink pad.
And oh, my *imprimatur*, to overhear you talk me,
like a gosling unsteadily imprinting—
it was nearly my undoing!

Suddenly I'm aware that everyone
everywhere is talking us, *mon amour*.
We've become the rumour of each other
and that rumour's growing, picking up momentum
like a meteor coming for me.
Already in the swelling shadow
of its all-consuming darkness
I'm disappearing like a mid-century politician,
because what's love but a Molotov cocktail
of what has and hasn't and has yet to happen
and ten thousand times as strong as anything you never tell me.

The Future Scene

I don't care and someone else should see if they can guess
a name for tricks the past plays on the mind.
The inescapable grid after the game of chess.
Or when forgotten frozen scenes long dead
play back like ghostly answering machines
in a sudden power surge to bend the pulse
and break a sweat as if time had broken loose
and run back to dig up a buried thread.

As for the future scene that from the blue returns
ensorcelling the soul to heedlessly possess
the incandescent body of the present,
I propose the name of love, one more for the list
of words the clear-eyed Eskimo devised
for that which when you touch it melts and burns.

Cut and a Blow Dry

("Tu ne me vois jamais, Pierre")

"I'm in love," I tell you.
I'm watching you watch me
in the mirror that covers the whole wall,

like one of those vast fading maps at the Vatican,
and always reminds me of a Greek trireme,
or an essence, how anyone ever got it

into this bottle of a shop front in the first place
where, through the battering gales
of the four winds from the blow dryers,

you're always telling me to fall in love,
as if it were up to me,
and you're always in love,

as if you were the poet.

"Poetry," you never cease to delight
in repeating, "Poetry
is not good for you. It turns you—"

but it's your hand that's turning
as you comb my wild, distracted hair
the way you always do, as if you're

listening so intently it doesn't matter
what we're saying
or how fast our conversation's racing,

[9]

or even when it seems to stop completely
in its tracks, like time never does
while we're still in it,

"too serious. *Troppo Serio!*"
We laugh together in the mirror.
There is no difference between us.

"And someone has died."
Your shears fall open, inconsolable,
beyond the naked flesh of my left ear,

your mouth stretched like melting plastic
into a *Commedia dell'arte* of grief.

"*Nobody* calls it a *beauty parlour* any more!"
I have once again performed unspeakably hopeless to a turn.
You are the patron saint of patience. "It's a *salon.*"

But that always makes me think of Paris
and bad painting, and I've come here to listen to you,
only you, talking to me, the two of us

adrift inside this bottled storm
blowing in from the four corners of the map
immortalising everything behind us.

Boy

Years before, the infant Salome had a favourite
she called Boy. He was always there, wrist-first,
heel-first, a hatless lassoed cowboy
dragged through girlhood's surface-of-the-moon
terrain, kissing the cliff-face of her bed, his mouth
around her hair, and, knowing he was hers,
belonged exclusively to her, she loved him.

Love was not enough or she would never have lost
Boy, naked, nameless, stupid and alone, beneath
a Waldbaum's sky coffered in coffee-stained
acoustic tile and hyperlit like human skin under
the microscope of teenage lust, under the shadow
of the precipice down which, split and paired
and glistening exactly like the sometime necks
of smallish animals or great big birds, molten
pomegranate rivers ran.

Back home she turned merciless. She snapped
the head off every last doll she possessed
and heaped the headless bodies on her bed.
She wept longer than anyone ever wept
and every night she dreamed of Boy,
only of him, his moulded-plastic head
mouldering in the dust of crates and cabbage leaves.

This, to satisfy those for whom cause and explanation,
and not the simple disposition of parts, is paramount.

The Speed of the World

There are gears in the air
and under the ground.
Discs without dimension.

Wheels with spikes
and wheels with cleats like teeth
alternating and inverting

night and day
like crenellations—
a veritable Caernarfon of fearsome rings!

They interlock, as gears ought to.
Like the man who hears
a voice from the past over his shoulder,

they're always turning.
And they govern the speed of the world.

The speed is constant. It never varies,
never slows. It never changes.
That should make it easy to fix

like the north star
and like the summer sky, easy to master.
I can't tell you why it isn't.

I take its measure, judge my entrance, I leap in—
but I don't land true.
Impact always stops me cold

or sends me spinning,
too in love with my own velocity
or sunk in leaden-legged labours.

It's sometimes days before I come to my senses.

And everywhere I turn I meet
a hundred blithe and busy creatures
credo the pace is theirs to set and keep,

and ten among them who daily drink
the frothing cup,
convinced they taste the tang of nectar.

And here's me
pounding the thick glass walls
shouting, *Fish!*

Just think about a Bach cantata,
the inscribed anatomy of Leonardo.
Can't you see why it goes so hard with me?

Once in a dream I believed I was the thing of art itself.
When I woke up I wasn't even the dreamer.

Pointless

When you leave the room, though it seems empty
and cold suddenly, the way it can, the weather
notwithstanding, and so pointless I
wind down like a mechanical clock, every breath
another second slower, and everyone bores me,
most of all the ones with souls who sweat,
rubbing their two sticks so hard with no hope of fire
I can taste eternity, it isn't death.

When you show up, I don't come alive,
Coppelia-like, all six senses sputtering
like the kettle in the morning, stuttering
like the boy with a conscience at the story's start,
and leap across the room in emulation of
my heart my heart my heart my heart my heart.

Variations on a Theme by Lady Suwō

Pillowed on your arm
only for the dream of a spring night,
I have become the subject of gossip,
although nothing happened.

Pillowed on your dream,
I come and go all spring,
taking pleasure in gossip
as though nothing happened.

Pillowed on my arm,
I confide only in myself
the dream of your arm,
my endless dream of your arm.

Pillowed on my dream,
I no longer drift out into a spring night
but make plans before sunset,
as if something happened.

Pilloried by love
I sip the dram of gods
from the spring of night—
Where's the harm in that?

Pillowed on the dream of your arm,
a mute owl on a bare bough
in a starless barn
shrouded in snow.

Disarmed by a spring night,
powerless against dreams,
assailed by gossip,
I throw the windows open.

Pillowed on the spring night
of your arm—
I can't sleep!

Pillowed on the gossip of your arm
I have become an object of ridicule
in my own eyes.

Pillowed on your *nothing*,
only for the dream of a spring *nothing*,
I have become the subject of *nothing*,
although *nothing*.

Pillowed on *his* arm
all night, all spring,
that the gossip may reach even to your dreams.

In my dream I am pillowed on your arm
and the clouds of a spring day
keep changing faster than gossip
or an emu running backwards.

Although nothing happened,
nothing happened
that hasn't already happened again.

[16]

Also noting happenstance.
Alto notes sing half steps.
Altered knots have ends.
All through knowing happiness.

Like the subject of gossip
as it begins to spread,
I keep your pillow
between my legs.

If nothing happened,
why has my pillow become
harder than your arm?

You
and your pillow
and your arm
and your dream
and your spring night
and your gossip.
As if.

L'oreiller de ton nez
que pour une belle nuit d'été
je suis devenue sujet
de ce rien qui n'est passé.

A Pillow, a Dream and an Arm
walk into a bar . . .

It wasn't your arm.
It wasn't spring.
It wasn't night.
It wasn't a dream.
It isn't gossip.
Nothing never happens.

night, spring, dream
of gossip
for on
the arm
a Pillowed
happened
your only I
become
the have nothing subject of
although . . .

Although nothing happened,
I have become the subject of gossip,
only for the dream of a spring night
pillowed on your arm.

Cliché

We often hear it said that there is
nothing quite so tragic as the innocent
death of a child, the terrible suspense

of so much colour. And I would not
gainsay it. It is not for me to weigh
the lead of suffering against the feather

of joy. But there are, too, the curious
averted deaths, than which there is
nothing sadder, which would have ended

in the tragic loss of such great promise
and by a morbid twist of noncommittal fate
greyly unwind and peter out and none the wiser.

The Yellow Dress

Inevitable city, coming back to you, like dreaming.
It all seems real.
I take for granted that it's half invented.
The headlong wind that brings on restlessness.
The bridge that vanishes halfway across the river.

Memories sleep and wake.
In between them I am drifting.
I know it's not that other summer's evening.
I recognise the past—it's nearer,
it's more vivid. The yellow dress
thrashing on the line
in the convent dormitory courtyard.
My Romanian roommate delirious with fever.
The day I skipped class—
like there was nothing to prevent me—
and we drove to the Camargue
to take in its "unique and savage landscape,"
according to you and your *Let's Go*.

The tall glasses of *pastis*.
The high late light. The chairs.
I slipped past but I took note,
you wanted to kiss me.
What followed after was unprecedented.

Hymn
before a bust of Sappho

Immortal Aphrodite, though in your eyes
neither mercy nor the hunger of desire
can be detected, since they lie in your head
like the impress of a leaf in snow,
at full tilt you are riding here now,
the wings of your sparrows in my ears beating,
my heart demented and refusing to heed me.
I can see you will not be deterred.

So I implore you, Dread Goddess,
since you turn your cold ear to my tormented lips,
inspire me to your likeness in marble
that no one can see through me
and never, never in a thousand years guess
the conversations that keep running with him in my head.

The Little Death

When I played Thisbe in eleventh grade
Miss Wilhelmina Penrest, up to then
my favourite English teacher, chose
John O'Leary, my own secret Pyramus,
to play the part of Pyramus. I loved
to study him each afternoon in Study Hall
framed like a print of the daydreaming Keats
in a small gap among the stacks which I had
delicately engineered. He was my first
pair of blue eyes—two pale blue shallow pools
the fairest shade of late July chlorine.
He had such pasty Irish skin, a fog
of wiry hair, that empty-headed grin.
Maybe she knew. Though she asked Henry Mersey
to play Wall, almost as keen to have me kiss
the chink his fingers made as I was loath
to do it. And what possessed her to press
Sally Wayne, who shone through acne craters
every time that Henry Mersey like the sun
came in the room, to take the part of Moon?
All this I could forgive. Although she very nearly
lost my love for good when to play Lioness
Miss Penrest picked that fizgig Helen Rosemount-Hill.

Rehearsals were a daily agony.
With every sally Henry Mersey made
I'd shrink and Sally Wayne would wax with hope.
And every time I sought John out, there was
that Helen Rosemount-Hill beneath her heap
of auburn hair, all set to pounce. Between
that and the way that Henry Mersey had

of mercilessly being in the way,
as if he understood things like a god
and not a wall, or else had spent a lifetime
in the office of a wall, immured
to human suffering, and so a god,
a very genius of a wall,
I couldn't get anywhere near John O'Leary.

I did believe things couldn't get any worse
than having to endure the Lioness
offer to read my part (my part!) with Pyramus.
Poor John, he never was that swift, still tripping
on his lines and cues and props, but did
he have to take her up with such alacrity?
It burned the way I wished that bloody sword
had it been steel and not collapsible on touch
would burn when every day I plunged it in my breast.
It didn't help that, all along, as I could tell
from how Miss Penrest flipped the pages
of her book and tapped her fingers with her pen
and fiddled with her glasses on their chain,
I was still falling short of Thisbe.

I still don't know why I went back.
I didn't need my script, I knew my role.
I was already late. It was getting dark.
I hated the smell of that auditorium.
I almost didn't hear the mobbled knocking
from the stage and turn to see the art department's
masterpiece, Old Ninny's tomb, shuddering
like the haunches of a fly-beleaguered cow,

[23]

the half unpainted mulberry banging,
doggedly, the papier-maché trunk beating
its bark like an indignant goose.

Next day when Henry Roughcast Wall accosted me
and offered me my book, I talked with him.
When Helen Lioness taught Sally Moon in France
it's called *the little death*, she paled and fled
in search of Thisbe to whom she confessed
that she had never even gotten to first base.
And when I, Thisbe, held both Pyramus
and John O'Leary limp and clammy in my arms,
and dead, and gazed down on that glist'ning brow,
where I counted eleven pimples and made out
in the corners of his mouth egg evidence,
I thought I could see what I was in for—
the foolish comedy of walls and moons,
the long succession of little deaths—
and I let Thisbe have her head, shaking
her fists, tearing her hair, beating her breast
in a spectacular display of deathless love,
until there was no more of that wretched fidgeting.

Alone in the Night

after Li Ch'ing Chao

Emergency rescue has just freed
the woman trapped for twelve hours
underneath the ice. As I drink
my peach schnapps, my hypothermia rises
in a fine vapour from my heart, streams
round the lonely peach stone of my cheek.
The room is unsteady, as if it were drunk.
I try to write a poem in which
two ice floes drift and dissolve like willows.
My cold cream has gone off.
My hairclip's yanked too tight.
I throw myself into my black bathrobe,
collapse back onto the gold couch and crush
the phoenixes in your *Peterson's Guide*.
A lone, deep ice cube chinks
like the last nickel lost in Atlantic City.
In the bitter loneliness of the window
I search for just one small watery
streak of day. Without even an old movie,
I lie changing channels in a blue light.

Three Ostriches

1

I know that from out there
there seems a lot to envy.
Legs long as summer afternoons
and quick as convertibles.
Feathers creamy and light
as French puff pastry.
But where there's stature
there isn't always depth.
Everything I know I've learned
from keeping an eye on the world
at the end of my periscope neck.
I lay gorgeous, enormous eggs
and hatch the most beautiful babies.

2

Oh! There are birds that can fly!
Birds with songs, that can sing!
Birds who write on water, glide
where I can only walk, or run,
as primitive as a man.
On the day I realised,
like a felled tree I collapsed,
my poor knees buckled back—
thump!—in a great roar of dust
like some defenestrated sack
for everything I know I lack.
On the next I hung my shingle,
Plumes for hats, for hire, for quills.

3

I know that from out there
with my feathers in the air
and my neck like a third leg
and my head like a spade
I might look a bit risible.
But don't buy the bad press.
It's not that I'm afraid.
I'm not hiding my head.
I'm giving it a rest,
getting it out of the heat,
letting my great bulk have a think.
I find treasures all the time.
And it's so wonderful to be invisible.

A Baroque Birdcage Seller
in the Seventh District of Vienna

When you wake me up with your trombone playing,
wanting me to pull the slide, and telling me,
even as you've told me many, many,
many times already, how you were classically trained
and *don't call it a sackbut, please,* I know
that soon we'll start to improvise, like the baroque
birdcage seller in that snow white winter
trompe l'oeil interior in the Seventh District
of Vienna, who readily persuaded us
that the cage was a three-tiered wedding cake frame
and the bird, hoodwinked and trussed to the trapeze,
would pipe up moreover presently again because
that way we'll come close, and find it harder to remember
what tune were you playing when you woke me up?

The Piano Tuner

You have to understand, it wasn't like it is today.
Back then there was the war and we believed in miracles.
Roosevelt was like a god, immortal.
And a visit from the piano tuner was an event,
looked forward to like Santa Claus here in America,
or a trip to the theatre.

In our family of musicians, no one ever touched Lolly's piano.
It was unspoken but forbidden.
Secretly, my sister and I longed to play it.
It rose up in the corner like a black iceberg,
opened for company: our Phantom Archaeopteryx
of folded wing and broken song.
The casket closed, it was austere as any tomb
even the name in mother of pearl
laid like a pale flower on its chest, down to the umlaut.

Until the day one of the aunts pulled out the bench,
sat down and produced the hysterical uproar that made us jump
like *Hic Haec Hochdeutsch* on our new RCA Victor.
And that's how it came about
that we were expecting a visit from the piano tuner.

For weeks my sister and I could think of nothing else.
He would come and everything would be altered.
We had such romantic ideas.
He would come and tune the piano to ourselves,
turn us and our wide-eyed passion all to music.
We lay awake in a state of expectation
like Dante's souls in limbo, or the children of Hamelin.

On the morning of the day of his appointment
my sister and I could hardly eat.
We were almost sick with anticipation.
In a dream, the clock struck the hour, the doorbell sounded.

But oh the creature who entered the front parlour!
He was half blind, with a squint, dwarf short, half lame
and he limped, which he somehow hid. And the tools
he dug up, pawing in his dead leather satchel,
were neither old nor worked; he handled them
without a trace of tenderness.
And the grovelling way he blinked,
rolling his head off at a crazy angle,
and the thick noises that came from his chest,
which made us think he might just turn and spit
on the parquet or ruin the antique Persian carpet.
And the furtive clicking in his throat before he spoke.
And the accent not too far from Father's.
And the tick tick tick of metal buttons on the wooden panels.

Afterwards there was no real reason to steer clear.
No one even called it Lolly's piano.
My sister and I had weekly lessons.
Every evening, after schoolwork, we took turns and practiced.
But it never sounded absolutely right.
Maybe it was the acoustics in the parlour.

And sometimes, just like that morning, even now,
I see the piano tuner, the bad leg of his trousers
hitched, the body riven from its lid, and hear
the sickening sound of tone moving
as he gobbles at his tongue and rummages,
peering over the side, in his con doctor's kit,
goring the dark innards, the dirty fingers of his fist
coiled about the shabby silver-plated idol,
as the piano, like an animal submitting,
turns to me its dull, unblinking eye of death.

Ceci n'est pas

The love letters you sent me were not love letters.
The nothings you whispered were not sweet.
The promises you promised were not promises.
Your kisses betrayed nothing.

The things you never wanted me to see
were not the things you didn't want me not to see.
You weren't the one I thought you were to be.
I was exactly what you expected.

The smoke that bellowed from the cinema
was not the fire that broke the paper moon.
The nest that piped its passion to the sea
was not the lookout gone to dream among the briars.

The lies you told me were not lies.
The truth that you professed was not the truth.
Love is not love and nothing is more real
than who we're not and what we never had.

Winter

on Martha's Vineyard comes on the ferry once a year, laden
with provisions and a sudden end to the general grumpiness
that's been on the upswell all summer. It always comes as
a surprise. We don't sink slow, gradually cooling, darkness
overtaking day by incremental bites, but plunge into sundown
before supper, ink-line trunks and dead-end branches.
Blizzards blossom out of calamine. I suppose some folks
might be vexed, but it's been our experience that heaven
tends to be more or less one step from Life as Usual. Life as
Usual. Life as Usual. Life as Usual, if The Season went sweet,
is December full of giddy summer money and everybody's
uncle. Bay windows glow in golds straight out of Rockwell.
Snow lies untroubled in our streets, the moulted skins where
traffic snaked and hissed all summer. The worried look of
shops is all soaped over, swirling fossils sunk in geologic sleep.
Behind the salt-sting, we unwrap our secret pearl cupped in
wintry palms of nacreous sky and sea and turn the world our
knuckled oyster shell. Otherwise, this is when everything
goes to hell. Last December, what with the rainy summer
and the dollar strong, calls in to the Tisbury police were up
precipitously—family disturbances, drunk and disorderlies.
Not that we talk about it much, but we all remember when
Mrs. —— spoke to nobody and wore her sunglasses in
Cronig's Market for a week. It may seem black and white,
but it's been our experience that if things don't go one way,
they tend to go the other. If you go up to Gayhead in January,
there is no one and nothing but the mechanical pulse of sea
pounding rock, just wearing it away, just eating it away. In
Oak Bluffs the carousel is boarded up, the brass rings stacked
and stored, and behind the paint-chipped gingerbread facades
and the porches worn like lacy aprons, all the dismal winter

little girls with dark hair and severe morals go merrily about their chores although they died a hundred years ago or more because they never got to play at house.

The morning is the hardest. It is morning

The morning is the hardest. It is morning
when I nearly don't remember. But I remember
once you said morning should come later,
which never made much sense, until this morning.

The middle of the day, my heart, reminds me
of a road I've never been on, it is endless.
The evening is the hardest, it's the darkness.
I count, and hide my eyes, until it finds me.

The hours fly off one by one, they leave without me.
I can't keep them and I can't see where they take you.

The night won't end and when you don't forsake me,
stroking my cheek, saying, "You can't come with me,"
it makes no sense, but then the sky is turning
and dark descending dawn dawns and it's morning.

Cross Country

Can you recall ever being so far west?
The hawks and even the sky they wheel about in
wilder than I've ever seen them.

But the farther west I travel, the less the country changes,
the more it feels like time itself unravelling.
Instead of taking it all in, I think maybe

I'm leaving myself behind,
and how can anyone tell the difference
between what they're learning and what they are unlearning?

And when does the past begin, anyway?
The last time I saw you
was that record-shattering beginning of July.

You were drinking from that bottomless bottle of water
you were always toting with you everywhere,
as if any minute you might find yourself

in some parched Mojave of the heart
with nary a compass, just outside Penn Station,
waiting for me.

I'd already been around the block,
only I made you believe we had been on the self-same train,
just come up two interchangeable exits.

And maybe that explains
how it is we spent the whole evening together
in two different places.

2

I am contending with a memory
and the memory is winning.

The smell of the end of summer
where swallows reverse and gather like shadows,

passion running like a dye
through the basin of frayed clouds,

even the stars we have in common,
none stronger than this memory

insistent as the bell in the mission outside Phoenix
like a firefly from my childhood.

And I can still feel the feel of the cold glass jam jar
with the punctured lid, the blind expectation

of that beacon's next occurrence
holding me with the strength of a man.

Maybe the desert is wherever we let go
and forget what we've already stopped believing in,

and why you were always ready for it.

3

The wild hawks circle and bob like a baby's mobile.
I have already begun thinking of them as my local angels.
They remind me of you looking after me from afar.

It's their God's-eye view—the fragile crossbar
that almost connects them with an end of string.
Watching their wings dip again before they level,

I half suspect the sky itself of tipping, and it's me
caught like a firefly in the ambiguity of twilight.
And often I talk to you, even though you're not here.

(It's when I don't recognise myself that I know it must be me.)
And when I answer, I know it's only another form of asking
the question not altogether captured by its answer.

Like the story you made up about us
when we couldn't find a place to set our picnic down,
your drummed-up native ancient lore conjuring forth

hawk-eyed Cherokee warriors,
how they'd find themselves a clearing after battle—
and I can still picture it, big and bright as a blue moon,

the prairie grass trembling like the lake of its reflection,
haunted by chieftains making peace with the enemy,
and because you told me, I believed it.

The Museum of Desires

Here are the thoughts you can't have
And here are the feelings you can't touch,
Melting like pictures you can't save
From burning buildings while you watch.

These are the loves you can't tell,
Locked in the quarry like ice in your veins,
Like beautiful lines you didn't spell
And beautiful scenes on a dark stage.

The hut from a past you can't name,
An exquisite shroud embroidered with rot.
An infant skull, the horn of a ram,
The relic's sacred martyred heart.

Here is an echo you can't hear.
Here is a cup and here are the kisses
Counted and numbered and bound and hidden
In secret vaults and shatterproof cases.

The Seamless Future

In the future, sidewalks won't have cracks,
not on purpose or from bad planning.
There'll be no thresholds: doors
will open out of walls like in old houses
with fascinating secrets, but without hinges.
No one will hesitate, wondering whether to go in.
No one will trip on grout or catch a heel
in gaps of cobble mortar—all the stumbles
will dissolve and fade from conversation.
Windows will obscure like walls, walls
clarify like butter, undetected.
In imitation of the ease with which dawn steals past
the most fanatic lookout every morning,
the made world will come to echo the given
until finally, in a perfect marriage of the natural
and the artificial, the world will be seamless.

And then our inner lives as if they were chameleons
and envious of the outer ones, will also even,
and love won't come in patches
but like whole cloth off the bolt,
mixed feelings blending like acrylics,
wisdom running ribbon
without frays or hitches, belief, desire,
inseparable from proof and gratification,
thought and action and reflection
no longer discrete acts of theatre, but like waters
lapping overlap until they deliquesce together.
Being in all ways as we seem to ourselves, seeming
to others just as we are, we too will be seamless.

Given time, even you and I will emulsify,
not remember where we end
or our beginnings, a continent at last, land
into water imperceptibly slipping, sea into ether.
The horizon won't have any.
There'll be nowhere to lay anchor.
Face and fathom, like hours,
like every disappearance, seamless.

The Accordion Player

He didn't actually have an accordion.
It was more the way he bellowed with his hands
splayed, as if he were God that clear May morning
unfolding like a fan, and only by chance
I'd come upon him wooing the controls.
He summoned the whole, down to the one cloud placed
like a beloved for the declaration of old.
It was not only the accordion to whom he played.
And I'll never forget that mercurial calm
as I followed the orbiting sails of his palms
in the seas of their mirrors like lovers approaching
where love lies hidden like nothing between them
but the pull and repeal that holds them and keeps them
apart and together, always never touching.

Land's End

The mist in the air and the not getting anything done.
I was reading the book I can never read without crying.
It's because the heroine doesn't know she's dying,
that he'll never leave her and she's not alone.

All day the breaking, breaking of the ocean
coming in like a voice in the gaps from ship to shore,
carving at the coast like the lips from the core
of a craving and sobbing like a deaf girl into a phone.

Like a castaway clinging to sand with arms of foam,
the sea cast a watery shadow on all that fading,
to- and fro-ing like a reedy widow waiting
for someone who isn't going to come home.

The mist in the air like the lack in the same dead dial tone.
The tangle of driftwood, the mangle of seagulls crying.
The sun like a Cyclops pierced by a cloud and dying
on all that is done and all that will never be done.

Leaving Eden

The motor's running and I'm leaving Eden.
It's gotten too small, too cramped. It's too green.
I've packed my bags, taken my best face cream,
shaken the apple tree until my wormy heart fell at my feet.

It's not the serpent. I didn't need convincing.
It's not in my nature to be happy to ignore what I know.
Can't remember when I first went suspicious.
If I'm disenchanted with the past at least I'm something,

something to the core.

There never was a paradise on earth, or heaven.
Each fleshy fist of fruit harbours its seed.
Nothing has changed, nothing was ever how it seemed
in Eden, and if it was, I can't imagine it was me.

The motor's running, the asphalt is seething.
My bare legs stick to vinyl slick with sweat.
The air of motion now will run its fingers through me
and like Atlantis underwater I'll forget.

Torture Garden

We'd rank Mozambique above Birmingham oxtails.
That's what I heard you say,
but the sound was so loud and the bass line booming
under the floor like a depth charge.

The wino drooping on that bench is Michelangelo—
and I thought I knew what you meant.
But the leaves were skating like a town in a Brueghel
and I couldn't think of everything.

You wore gloves after a thaw in the arboretum,
holding a salver in the Levantine manner,
unless it was your view of the river,
which at one time must have been sensational,

but by then it looked more and more like a wooden nickel,
the future frozen over, and all I wanted to know
was how to mix a blue zombie with triple sec
and if you could feel a numb cocktail going down.

Nature Morte

This has nothing to do with hunger.
That fruit's been sitting out too long.
That peachy cleft's delectable, but wrong.
That lemon is unpeeling like a stripper.
Each apple's been meticulously rotated
just like they do it in the supermarket
to hide bang-spots and worm-holes; the wicker jacket
on that demijohn is obviously dated.
Just touch that orange and it'll bruise black and blue.
Leeching up through the slathered layers of oil and wax,
the carcass-y fumes'll surface like low-tide sea-stink,
like envy in conversation. They lie
who say that it looks good enough to eat.
A still life puts me off my fruit at least a week.

The Clear Thread

The miracle of birth, the miracle of scalpels
and blood-soaked sponges, of the separation
of mind and body. It's just as well
that it's been finally accomplished.
And by something so simple—a curtain
to keep the gaze from the holy miraculous.

There was a time a labyrinth was required,
the circuitous routes angular and unforgiving
as the thinking of a liar,
to keep the brute brow of the body out of mind.
And at the heart of it the heaving Minotaur
to be kept in food but out of sight.

We were protected from him thus, and he from us.
So we progressed from myth to dream, from lie
to lie, from lie to unkept promises.
Even the bravest girls were too unwary.
Wise men hallucinated that their sons would fly
who are as flightless as the cassowary.

Welcome, welcome. Her arms pinned wide as Christ's
to mock at heaven as it drips and drips into
her waxen index finger. The anaesthetist
is from Hawaii. He says, incredulous,
you are crying to have a boy? Ferocity
like a god out of the machine billows

over the horizon and holds, a tethered bull,
and the play is done. The regular maddening
breathing of clouds and tides all around, scrub-blue,
powdery blue, resumes. The clear thread
takes up the stitch again, the beetling
brow of the surgeon glistens as he grips his end.

Theseus has killed the Minotaur.
The youth of Athens are set free.
The hero sails for home, his hand light on his father's sword,
beneath the accustomed black sheets, and doesn't dream
he doesn't understand what he has done, what he
has seen, while she, recumbent on her Naxos, sleeps.

Poppies

Sleep, oh I could sleep, but for the noise of fire,
the scorch and blaze of blaring scarlet
trumpeting, red bells hailing to the core—
Do they think they've got the sun for a clapper?

The thin-skinned whispering in this district
goes shudder to rot. Gaudy, by God, as bite-your-lip-
blood-red lipstick, the edges running, shredded,
quivering. That gash will scar, will not be stitched,

a mouth to mock the myth that madness is
a clarity of intellect, a crystal
architecture, thought succeeding thought.
Precisions gone too fine, too violent.

In this shrill field, this sick profusion
which is not far from the ordered yellow squares
patching the countryside like homespun quilts
where rapeseed flourish, blinding, in the sun,

the poppies burst like blisters, ruin the green.
They flare like London sprawling on the map.
They over-open like Ophelia's skirts
spreading to the borders like a dream,

dreamlike hold the light upon the water,
until they fill and pull the floater under.

Glass Bottom Car

Windows are overrated.
    I never liked fairs. Landscapes
like a ground bass, scene after scene.
        Auger bit developments. Mortis and beam.
            Oak elm pine white green bare trees.

The high streets, the highways,
    go felly round spokes. Celluloid living,
a wooden-maned horse. Film frames on sprockets
    cranked by telephone poles.
        Trick magic old-world lantern shows.

My windscreen was snow-blacked,
    bug-juice grimed. I didn't want windows.
I covered them up. The metronome wipers
    couldn't clean or keep time.
        When you've seen this world once it's enough.

I like to go fast
    in my glass bottom car, the macadam moonscape
is never the same, the cracks in the craters,
    they break my heart,
        on the coal-coloured lard milky way,

and never look up,
    watch the road rush black, rich river oil
torrents in hard rain, streamers riding the wind
    snapped and no way back
        in my glass bottom beauty machine.

A Sprig in a Cold Snap

Tired of falling out and in and out of love,
I woke up sure the dream of you had fled
some time since, like the negligent resolve,
a car alarm, a sprig in a cold snap,
leaving the clouds of our imaginary bed
the way the landing plane surrenders
the fancy of its airborne assumption
to the unstrenuous solidity of fact.
It was the lulling lure's legerdemain.
The waking was the dream, the interruption
that opened like the chasm between chapters
only to vanish in the ready page-turn
of compulsion and like the suppressed symptom
I see you now everywhere and with a vengeance.

True Love

There's no such thing except love at first sight.
I am in love with everyone I meet.

I'm not in love with anyone I know.
I fall in love every new place I go.

A fool for jackleg joints and lovesick streets,
I drift on purpose wantonly through districts

where the signs are down. And when I stick
to travelled-level paths, paths that retrace

comfortable covered ground, familiarness
chokes me like sense dead in my tracks, lays flat

every mirage of love, and that's the end of that.

Just so, each time I outstrip meet to crack
more than a tiny crack the box of know,

Pandora-like, spectacularly blow
restraint, smashing the seal, the hinge, the back,

to let the tide of feel drag me away,
I come up nothing left, except, for true love's sake,

to run (nothing when held, weak, cursed except to say,
I will be back I will you know I will).

The thing of love's a self-consuming snake.
The first kiss thrashes with the throes of end.

Don't tell me we'll escape that heaven of hell,
and for the sake of true love, I'll pretend.

The Affair

after Anonymous

1

We break every date in the diary.
Inside my inbox a hundred emails
bloom. There are tulips on the walls
in this hotel where we never run out
of things to say, your tongue in my,
my tongue in your, mouth.

2

The banks of the cloudless river
curve and sweat. The deep shade,
the sultry verge, the inside of your thigh,
the flesh of leaves, the flood of light
rising and falling across my emerald,
your jade, skin.

3

Headlights search the bus shelter
where the rain climbs
in a craquelure of greenhouse vines.
I peel at the corners of an old movie poster.
You warm my hand
in the hollow of your chest.

4

The annual Christmas party,
the endless winter. Fat pearls
of wax land on the red tablecloth,
spring rain on my tongue. Under
the blanket on the windowsill,
love letters in the snow.

The Dog and Duck

These sour old men would swiftly trade
ten years for what we have in mind to do.
It's too hot in this corner
and we've been here for hours
but you somehow haven't noticed
that our promiscuous parley,
how far do I go, which way should I take it,
is starting, bodily, to try my patience.

You've brought me to The Dog and Duck,
surrounded me with hunting pictures,
and I appreciate the gesture.
But all those men with guns behave,
the hounds are too well trained.
I can't stop staring at that bird
hanging in rapture,
a saint of Mannerism,
the S of her neck so lately rampant
all uncoiled, slaked, wrung,
eminent of every longing.

It's hard to breathe and hard to think
and I'm too coy and you're too charming
and then again my eye keeps straying
where those wild old men taking their rouse
keep braying, drinking the long week's end,
and how, unblinkered and unblinking,
they would trade a swift ten years,
and maybe more, maybe much more,
while you keep talking and my free hand in desperation
goes to hold the hair up off my neck but nothing helps.

[57]

This pub smells of dog, the doggy air is baying.
You're not shy but you're too literary
in this heat, and, in this heat,
which comes at me and comes at me—
I'm crushing out my cigarette.
I'm finishing my drink.
I'm licking my unliterary lips.

Tell me, my duck, how is it with you?
And, what, exactly, are you going to do
when I let slip
this low-cut high-heeled fishnet whore-hound kiss?

Proof

You stay away.
You sit beside me.
You have nothing to say.
You stay away.

You stay away.
You come round
Only to refute my supposition that
You stay away.

I'm profligate with my affection
But not with you.
I have nothing to say.

You make me wait.
You stay away.
Love is not susceptible to proof.

The Same Dream

Je t'aimais avant de le savoir.
— LES LETTRES DE VERLAINE

It's always the same dream,
I resume and it's recurring.
I've memorised the words
but it's always the rehearsal.

There's a searchlight, like a yearning;
like desire, each time it finds me
it burns whiter and like lightning
in illuminating blinds me.

Though I can't seize what I'm seeking
through the gap a window traces
in the wall of the partition,
I have been both places.

When the light dims it's night falling.
I have fallen, like a curtain,
on you dreaming the same dream
in a different country.

Here's Looking at You

I'm the dame, and you're the dick.
My eyes are greener than the new kid—
Why does he look so damn familiar?—
my legs are longer than the San Andreas Fault,
and it's a call, but it's my heart
that's flawed and hard and colder still
than all the loveless bodies hard-knock cops
fish from the star-crossed, moon-lorn Bay
and blacker than La Brea's blackest pit.
That's how you see me.

And I can see that you're about to pour
that bleak long inextricable worn look
stiffer than the drink you just passed up
into the endless pitch of my impenetrable Ray Bans.
You're screening *Stairs of Sand* again.
The old print ticks with fraying static threads,
the murky script rises and surfaces
out of a soundtrack thick as blackstrap with cliché
like fresh rot from the dark
where I'm the con and you're the mark.
I'm the kiss and you're the tell.
You're the how, I'm the why.
I'm the blinding booze, the sucker bet,
and you're the loner with the heart of gold,
that fatal yen for just the kind of trouble
you know better than to stick
your supersensitive neck out for
and in spite of which,
because there's no such thing as love,
because no one ever does anything for nothing,

because you can't even begin to figure out what the hell
you're doing here,

and I never asked you,
you won't stop until you save me.

Your Clouds

"My clouds! My clouds!" you exulted,
hurtling skyward, almost as if by pointing
you could disappear back into the hand
with which you were drawing
your cloud studies of the other morning.

And when I pointed downwards,
where we were standing,
you thought you could see to the bottom,
unless you were only seeing
those embedded stones that were your clouds.

The Catastrophe of the Old Comedy

While you were away, and you were always away,
that unbroken spell of white nights and eclipses,
small portents, strange hours, ghost kisses,
I often wondered if it was you causing them—the way
Prospero burst the heart of the sea—
by that sort of sympathetic magic that compels
the help of a spirit who must one day be dispelled;
and whether, unbeknownst to me, it was me.
Or whether it was simply me, in the cups of my ignorance,
judging things against nature that were merely real,
as a way of disarming my most brazen glances
into the chaos at the centre-less centre
until there was nothing that still seemed familiar
apart from the miraculous, and bad dreams.

It's Never Too Early for a Clean Slate

I'm still blinking at the clean slate of morning
and the voice by my head has been round the world already.
She reassures me like a baby, but I'm forty-two if I'm a day
and I need to hear the forecast,
which I still haven't learned has nothing to do with the weather.

My first cup scalds my lips, my gums, the parapets
and vaults of my mouth and you're talking to me
in the native tongue, which was my own once,
set like type or handprints in cement, as near
second nature as Mother Nature, but I can't make
heads or tails of anything you're saying.
Nevertheless I remain solidly convinced I only need to try
a little harder, apply myself with more stick-to-itiveness
to be able to save you, or be myself saved,
from what, from the look in your eyes,
is some not-so-new or even unforeseeable disaster.
If only I could hear myself think.
But I'd need earplugs and a pneumatic drill
to get through this concrete layer of words,
and your eyes don't even seem to hear me when,
out of time, ideas and desperation, I semaphore
in my own dead language and remember my father
saying never fall in love with a foreigner,
in the middle of the night he'll curse you.

But it's only first thing in the morning,
and not the first time, by my troth, I've failed to seize,
let alone shuck, a pearl of wisdom cast like an aspersion before me,
and time to go, so I wave good bye,
which I see is an ambiguous, as well as an ambidextrous, gesture,
but at the same time I also can't see—
and what choice do I have?
I don't have two right hands.
But the coast is clear, the toast is cold,
we're at the crossroads of the breakfast table.

And it's not until after I unbolt the chain, let slip
the wards of God, or Whoever it is Whose gates these are,
and toss precaution, and my only set of keys,
into the hedge, that I notice
that it really isn't too early yet
and I'm brimming with hope,
which has its disadvantages.

Frankie, Alfredo,
after Catullus XVI

I'll give you some of your sour grapes to suck on,
since you suspect my poems only sell because
I tart them up like high school girls in Camden.
A real poet must live in stripy jumpers
and two pairs of glasses, eschew irony
and mascara, and tend countrified passions
lest helpless young men divagate or query
their maudlin eds. and over-the-hill tutors,
whose backs are stiff and abacuses rusty
(hence their tendency to curse their barstools, beat
hendecasyllables with lifeless digits),
why they have to pickle their rhetorical
figures in the formaldehyde of bitters.
And you, full of voluptuous objection,
because my verses spill over with push-up
bras and low-riding tangas think I'm a girl!
Name the dawn. I'll take your mouths and your money
both hands tied behind my back, in a blindfold
and ten bona fide inches of stiletto,
one after the other, or both concurrent,
and no seconds. We'll just see who's left standing.

Self-Portrait as Myself

Oh, I've done Socrates and Jesus Christ
off the cuff and, not above a touch of theatre,
Lady Macbeth, with a nod to Ellen Terry.
I confess to smoke and mirrors, stand-ins
like those palindromic Annas, Emmas,
Pips, and Ottos, innocent and flawed
but somehow so convincing
even I have fallen for them.
I've pulled off my beard,
tossed my hat onto the table
and put up that sign that reads:
    No Signs
appending the unequivocal rider:
No Pipes No Pauls No Pigment
No Semaphores Allowed No
Subtle or Unsubtle Gestures
No Fancy Pared Down Back-Formed
Greco-Latin Nomenclature
to become The Allegory of Myself—
a naked canvas, blood-smeared, nerve-
strung, gut-impastoed—stepped back
to see, for myself, if it was true,
and it was honest as the morning,
it beggared blunt, and so revealing
it thundered like the cavalry with feeling,
fraught to flooding, full to death of meaning.
But it wasn't me.

And since you've come for me
I offer you myself instead,
today, in the image of my dead grandmother—
among my better efforts.
She's in one of her beloved caffs,
Vienna, between the wars,
a back room, gilt and mirrors,
a proscenium of smoke, a fox
dangling from a chair-back
like a provocative suggestion.
Dark and small, in classic
clingy Vionnet, back and shoulders bare,
in quarter profile, turning,
already laughing, already
demurring, her rosewood
scrolls of hair that could have been carved by Gibbons,
a woman of absolutely no convictions
but one or two political connections
(eventually they save her),
who never reserves judgment,
who loves cards
(in fact she is a gifted player),
but whose real genius is for flirting.
She does it all the time, with everyone.
She does it here, in my self-portrait.
Come close, you might catch her even now
regarding her reflection like a man.

Transcriptions of Éluard

On the day of the eclipse, when time collapsed
midnight into noon and we stopped, along
with every moving thing and every growing thing
upon the living surface of the shadowed planet,
we proved beyond the shadow of a doubt
we still believed in something like a God
enough to still believe what turned its back
staked all our love against indifference.
And all day under the spell I remembered
the eager boy that summer in Avignon
delivering transcriptions of Éluard on blue paper,
how carefully he began to dress, and your long hair,
and how I used to navigate the corridor as if I always wore
a careless coy chignon in hot weather and take no notice.

Poetry Lover
after Catullus X

"I was innocently perambulating the poetry section
when your *cavaliere* fell upon me like a sword."
Varus had been telling me about him ever since we'd met,
and while they bandied the ins and outs of an indecorous word
which one of them had lately come upon, his eyes
roaming my *Campus Martius*, his mouth
wrestling the smile that sputtered and flickered
like a dodgy filament into submission,
I inferred the wattage of his intelligence.
And it was then I noticed his hands,
which were rather small, and clever,
like a couple of Marx brothers,
and which even seemed to be pacing,
black cuffs flapping behind them like coattails,
and how much I liked the seemingly uncalculated mix
of reticence and daring
when he sidled in between myself and Varus.
We exchanged some *à propos*
that quickly transposed into repartee—
the poetry scene in the States
where he had just been promulgating
his most recent prize-winning collection,
how well it was selling, how handsomely
they'd paid him for his university readings,
especially at Harvard;
his American hosts, how well-off they were
and the preposterous show they'd made
of merely subsisting on their intellectual shoestrings,
eschewing red meat and pumping iron
almost as remorselessly as they pumped him
for particulars of Life in England;

putting him up at the home of the chair
of the English department.
You stayed with Harry Levin?
Our eyes locked, his glittering with a pleasure
I had come perilously close to wanting to learn the inside of.
I didn't expose him for a fraud and an impostor
(Harry Levin being dead these eighteen years),
but it wasn't long before I broke it off with Varus
and swore off the whole perfidious breed,
since male poets can't seem to tell the difference
between lies of art
and the delicate exigencies required when speaking with a lady.

Now Blue, Now Green

Somewhere there are twelve children playing in a field.
Somewhere there are twelve children playing in a road.
Each of the children has a name and is nameless.
Each of them has a mother and father and is orphaned.
Each has seen the sky and bitten through a blade of grass
yellow or green as the rain proposed.
Each has saved a beetle from murderous hands
and murdered a beetle with a placid crack.
Each has flown the flight of the fly, with its buzz,
and a fighter plane, and a buzzard.
Each has said one thing and thought another.
Each has said one thing and meant another.
Each has said nothing and thought nothing and been nothing.
Each has thought, "I am a cloud. I am thunder. I am a beetle,"
running down the field, or the road, chasing a ball.
Each has made a world disappear,
seen another rise up out of oceans to meet it.
Each has seen one piece of grass become a field.
Each has gone from standing in the wood
to pinching one leaf in a road.
We are always falling through the road onto the field
or out of the field into the road.
Twelve children chase a ball.
There are twenty-four children.
The children chase the ball,
half red, half yellow, now blue, now green,
that gets away from them and rolls.

Jigsaw World

Ten thousand pieces. So I don't suppose
there's any reason to start another.
But having put the whole damn thing together, we're at loose ends.
We did expect at least the feeling of having done,
something, accomplishment, some finished sense.

It's taken months and weeks, overtaken
all our daylight hours, taken over our dreams,
making the pieces fit, the knobby bits
like heads, snapping them in
their slots, like guillotines designed for them.

Our hands still grip the ghosts of all those manikins
as if—but what could come of those incipient limbs?
Our minds have started to play tricks.
Chairs slip under tables with a click.
If we were in them, there we sit.

The pillows in our made-up beds fit or don't fit.
The outlines all around us hitch, unhitch.
Remember Plato's hiccupping symposiast, his speech
of lover and beloved split, that puzzling itch
until Eureka relinks each to which? That was the myth.

It's just like this. So civilized. So east to west
that we can't bring ourselves to break it all to bits.
In the beginning it seemed impossible and rich,
like two-man skiffs dragged up onto the sand at midnight lit
by open fires, the glowing skin of boar on spits.

Instead, this map, its pat illusions, heights and depths.
The world again the way it was before Columbus, flat.
I can see round every corner, front and back.
All things that once swelled big at the edges end.
The pieces of the world are but themselves.

Ditchdigger

*If one's years can't be better employed than
in sweating poesy, a man had better be a ditcher.*
— LORD BYRON

I have a friend who has a friend whose father dug ditches,
which my friend had to admit he never had.
"A hole, sure, deep and wide enough to accommodate
a substantial root system, transplant
a good-size yard-shrub maybe. But a ditch, that's
something different. A ditch takes hours,
takes a man into the ground up to his shoulders.
You don't get strong from ditchdigging,
and you don't get healthy, but like my friend
likes to say, 'One thing's certain
when you get up every morning to dig a ditch:
you know where you are. My father'd always say,
*The day I stop digging ditches'll be the day
they find me in one I was very nearly done with.*' "

Hooks and Buttons

Like meeting someone you once used to know
or any ordinary moment the next day
or stepping in your own prints in the snow
or saying the same words you always say,

buttons, no matter how adroit you sew,
or if you found the one that got away,
never go back in the same place, just so
a hook and eye once parted always stray.

But if all time were a fantastic coat
teeming like waters in a fishing bay
with every button ever gone afloat
and every hook or eye to disobey,

like diamonds in a velvet-covered drawer,
I'd wear it to the bottom of the road,
the clever fish that never learned to roar,
the big mistake the experts never caught,

and all of me a hook far from the terror
beyond the tender mouth of Plato's cave,
a starless black alight with shooting stars,
and every other fabulous escape.

Archimedes and Me

It's the morning after the deluge
and I'm walking down Northern Boulevard
just past the LensCrafters (or is it a Pearle Vision?)
when I have this great idea for a movie.

It opens on you and me, Archie,
or two people just like you and me,
walking down Northern Boulevard—and I,
the way they say Balzac composed, pacing,

start speaking one part, then the other,
back and forth, back and forth—
and the one who's like me turns
to the one who's like you and says,

"I have this great idea for a movie,"
and the one who's like you turns
to the one who's like me and says, "Yes?"
in that mock-indulgent tone you adopt

whenever you don't want me to know
how adorable you find me, and the one
who's like me says, "Yes," as if she
hasn't noticed that he's looking at her

like a proof-reader scanning the final proofs
for that something that has so far
eluded his notice. "It's about us,
or two people just like us, and one of them

[78]

comes up with a great idea for a movie
and the other one makes like he's sceptical,
but he isn't, really; really, he's every bit
as keen as she is." And as the one who's

playing me is telling the one who's playing
you, he gets that sceptical look on his face
that, when you get it, really means you're
remembering something we were doing

last night, or imagining something
we may be doing later, but the one who's me
just forges ahead, laying it all out until she's done.
Then she turns to the one who's you and says,

"So what do you think?" And he turns to her
and says, "That sounds like a great idea."
And she says, "Really? Do you really think so?"
And he says, "Yes. I really think so.

It sounds like a very good idea indeed."
And she says, "Are you sure? Are you really sure?
You don't seem sure." And that's when I step
in a puddle the size of a bathtub

so that I have to take a step backwards
to avoid getting both feet wet,
and that's when I remember, just as when
I really am talking to you, I'm talking to myself again.

Le Mot Juste

The dresses lit up in the window at Bonwits
the winter I turned eighteen are still there.
Like a burr in my hair the grip of them sticks.
The pattern and fall of the skirts still hold fast,
not like leaves, or a kiss, or the green in the thread
of medieval tapestries, which don't last.

And here the word lodged like a blank in my head,
the one no thesaurus will ever repair,
like the plane tree the council slated for chips,
an immovable stump I keep stumbling against,
or one of those bold *idées fixes*, or a drunk
on a bench fulminating at himself.

When I remember it's not just a myth,
le mot juste, like that once-fabled creature
preserved in the Fifth in a pen and blue leaves,
or the life I spent half my life dreaming I lived,
I catch on a longing I used to resist,
the winter, that window, and how it was lit.

Dedication

Remember that vase?
The one on the hearth? That beautiful white
antique repeating pattern from Granada?
The one wound round with eglantine.
I always loved that flower. The one
we thought we'd never get home intact,
or anywhere else for that matter,
once we had found the flaw—*remember?*—
the quiet fracture of the evermore
about-to-last-forever
crash of imminent disaster. The one
we've had as long as we have had
each other, and all the things we saved
within the bell of its accommodating darkness—
lost now, though most I still remember.
Do you remember the man who sold it to us?
How he went on and on? You said
so he wouldn't have to listen to demurrals
and excuses of cornered window shoppers,
and I'm not sure the same could not be said
for why some stay silent.

Remember that vase.
I hope you'll remember, because
this morning, though I couldn't tell you what,
something appeared to me so irretrievable
I resolved there was simply nothing for it
but to rearrange the vase. It was, I think,
the way it sat there like a record skipping.
It didn't slip. I held it to my lips
a good long time before I let go.

[81]